T0128875

Thinning

with the

Angels

A Journey of Adversity to New Life

iUniverse, Inc.
New York   Bloomington

Thinning with the Angels
A Journey of Adversity to New Life

iUniverse books may be ordered through booksellers or by contacting:

iUniverse
1663 Liberty Drive
Bloomington, IN 47403
www.iuniverse.com
1-800-Authors (1-800-288-4677)

Because of the dynamic nature of the Internet, any Web addresses or links contained in this book may have changed since publication and may no longer be valid. The views expressed in this work are solely those of the author and do not necessarily reflect the views of the publisher, and the publisher hereby disclaims any responsibility for them.

ISBN: 978-1-4401-1694-0 (pbk)
ISBN: 978-1-4401-1695-7 (ebk)

Library of Congress Control Number: 2009923630

Printed in the United States of America

iUniverse rev. date: 3/03/2009

To Jerry,
whose constant love and support has helped me to
reclaim the joy life offers

Acknowledgments

No dream happens in isolation. It takes the love and support of many people to bring an idea into reality. I would like to thank:

My best friend of twenty years Cindy Bremeier for her unselfish love, which I will treasure always.

Sister Jo Casey, whose daily prayers and love brought the healing of God and the angels to me.

Dr. Cindy Solliday McRoy for the gift of her professional skills and consistent companionship and for helping me focus on what is essential in life.

The Bariatric Surgery Clinic of Froedert Hospital in Milwaukee, Wisconsin, headed by Dr. James Wallace and assisted by Debbie, Nedra, Keri, and Amy.

Father Kenneth Omernick for graciously granting me the time I needed for healing.

The Community of St. Gregory the Great Church, especially the Tuesday morning scripture group who pray continually for my success and health, and the Pastoral Staff, especially Kathy Luty and Gina Kuemmel, whose hospital visits and walking regime challenged me to get well and back to work as soon as possible.

My sister Josie and my friends Carmon and Nelda who were—and continue to be—great cheerleaders as I continue my journey toward a healthy weight and new life.

Susan Pittelman for her guidance, patience, and creative ideas of how to turn my dream into a reality.

Dr. Mag, who spoke with compassion and care and finally broke through to my heart and gave me courage.

Carolyn Kott Washburne, my editor, whose enthusiasm and support guided me to see the value of my work.

To God for the gift of new life.

Contents

Introduction

Addiction is a wicked disease. Regardless of what a person is addicted to, this menace can strip a person of self-worth and inner peace. Addiction tells a person lies about what truth is and depends on fear to keep its grip on a person's dignity. As pain deepens, the addict increases the attempt to make the pain go away. As the addiction increases, the person digs a hole deeper and deeper until it seems he or she can never climb out. Things get so bad that the only way to see is to look up. Despair can lead one to prayer and recovery or it can lead one to a mental hell that destroys the joy of life. It takes courage to seek the good and be committed to moving forward.

I am an addict. My addiction is food. I have been running from the truth of my life since I was very young. My long distance run brought me to four hundred pounds and a very unhealthy life. During this experience I have encountered many people who have been callous and cold to obese people. I have met many judgmental people who believe that the morbidly obese choose to be morbidly obese, just as alcoholics choose to drink and workaholics choose to work. Many believe that people want to be unhappy. This just isn't true.

Thinning with the Angels is the story of my journey of seeking the truth in my life and claiming the joy of life that is the right of every human person. It is a story of truth laid out for those who are suffering from feelings of poor self-esteem and worthlessness.

It is also a story of hope. It is a story of love. It is a story of challenge. It is a story of God's grace manifesting itself in the struggles, in the prayers, in the love of family and friends. It is a story of God's Divine providence and love for all people as seen in the angelic aid that God provides through those special beings with or without heavenly wings.

It is my hope that those who read this story are filled with hope. It is my prayer that those addicted will reach out for the help they need and seek support from family and friends to claim life again. It is my hope that those who read this story, and are not themselves addicted to any life-strangling disease, will grow in compassion for those of us who struggle every day to choose the good.

May you find in these pages the gift of new life.

Chapter One

Angels All Around

I'm not an expert on angels. My first recollection of angels was when I was very little and went to religion classes on Saturday mornings at our Catholic church. We were taught the **Guardian Angel Prayer: Angel of God, my guardian dear, to whom God's love commits me here. Ever this day be at my side to light and guard, to rule and guide. Amen.**

As a child I remember the holy card that Sister gave us. The scene was very peaceful. There was a large, loving angel with huge wings bending over and protecting two little children as they crossed a bridge over a brook. It was a symbol of how much God loved us and that we could always count on our angel being with us to protect us from anything evil.

I have to confess that I didn't really have any interest in angels as I was growing up. I don't think I was conscious of their existence. In fact, if anyone were to ask me if I wanted to see an angel, I would have freaked out. Those spirits, whoever and whatever they are, could keep their distance from me. I didn't need any heavenly visitations.

Then the television series *Touched by an Angel* became popular. Although Andrew, the Angel of Death, still frightened me, Monica seemed to be a loving and caring angel with one primary message to share. Monica was to let people know that God really loved them and that they could change their lives if they wanted to. Every episode showed the conflict of good and evil and how God's love was strong enough to defeat evil. This was the extent of my knowledge and interest in these heavenly messengers. I heard people talk about angels and admired their collections of angel things. Many of my friends had angel statues, pins, tote bags, and many, many books and pictures. Many times I would just tolerate their show-and-tell-sessions. When they talked about their experiences with angels saving them from disasters, I either dismissed what they were saying or nodded my head and let them ramble on. I very seldom listened to what they said. It was more than I cared to focus on.

Calling on the Angels

Then one day during a psychotherapy session, my therapist asked if she could share some "chi" energy with me. She happened to be a Reiki Master. I remember feeling very blocked inside. I was unfamiliar with Reiki and what this process was meant to accomplish. The therapist asked a few questions about where I felt I was at, but I didn't feel that I could really respond to the questions she was asking. I knew I had much to say but couldn't put my thoughts into words. I agreed to the energy process, not exactly knowing what it all meant. I hadn't heard of "chi" before. She explained it was the flow of energy through one's body that allows a person to be in balance.

I closed my eyes and could feel the movement of her hands around me. As she moved her hands over my head and face and around the top of my head, she mentioned the names of the archangels Michael and Raphael. She touched my shoulders. As she placed her hand on my left shoulder, she called upon Michael to protect me as I journeyed through the issues of my life. Then, placing her right hand on my right shoulder, she invoked Archangel Raphael to heal what was broken and scattered in my heart. I was scared, but I prayed that God would give me the openness to gain healing from this process. It was at this point of this session that I experienced something I have never experienced before.

There was a rush of energy beginning at the top of my head that swirled itself around me and through me like rushing water. I could feel movement through my throat and chest. I felt stuck. The doctor asked me to identify where I felt the blockage and I did. I could feel heaviness in the center of my chest that radiated down into my abdomen.

With more prayer and hand movement I could feel the blockages release as the energy flowed from my head and throat to my abdomen and through the rest of me until it seemed as if my feet wanted to explode. I could feel movement within my whole body. The image was like rushing water as it cascades down rocky falls. Then I felt surrounded with warmth that I could only identify as love. Finally, I experienced a deep sense of calm and I felt filled with the power of God.

This was my introduction to the angels. Michael and Raphael, two angels I had mentioned in my official prayers, were just angels with names until I experienced their power and presence. In response to this experience I started to explore just what and who angels are and how they could possibly help someone like me.

Why the Therapist?

I think it's only fair to tell you why I was seeking help from a therapist. I am a very obese person. I have a number of health issues that cause me to be on medications. Some of these medications make it very difficult for me to lose weight. However, there is more to the dilemma of weight retention than medications. It would be too easy to blame it all on pills. I came to the understanding that I needed help in coming to terms with why I make the choices I make when it comes to food. Food has become a comfort to me. When I feel sad or rejected, tired or stressed, my innards churn and I think I'm hungry. Even after I eat, there is still something that leaves me feeling empty.

I know now that it isn't a hunger for food—it is a hunger for myself. I am seeking to know myself, be myself, and love myself. It is a hunger to know the divine that is within myself. I am only now coming to realize that the emptiness I experience at times … the raw, burning desire to know more … is really my heart and soul reaching out to the power that is above me … the power that surpasses me. I call this higher power **GOD**.

The decision to see a therapist was a hard one. Was I now too weak to try to lose weight on my own? Was I one of the "crazy" folks who couldn't figure life out on my own? I knew that I was not doing so well on my own, so I needed to look at a new reality that opened my eyes to see that I did need some professional help.

God and His Angels

I have always been a religious person. I have always believed in God. But I didn't think much about the fact that God has angels. These heavenly beings surround God's throne and sing God's praises. Sounds like an easy existence. However, according to what we read in the Bible, angels have also been given a variety of tasks to do as well. Angels are assigned to help us as we walk our life journey. That means they are called upon by God to help every one of us.

Angels are present to guide us in our decision making. Angels are messengers of the Divine sharing the message of God's love with us humans. The word "angel" means "messenger". Angels are called upon to protect us from the possible evils of the world, and although angels cannot force us to choose rightly, they can pray for us that we will. Our freedom to choose to do right or wrong remains intact even with the presence of these angelic beings. Angels pray that we choose to be the best human beings we can be so that we will eventually experience salvation and enjoy the vision of God that the angels themselves enjoy.

There is, however, one catch to this angelic intercession experience. Angels can do nothing for us unless they are invited into our lives. Unless we open the door to these divinely created spirits, angels can only stand by us and watch. We need to ask for their assistance. I found this difficult to do because I am not a person who can easily ask for help when I need it. I guess I would say I am very independent and self-sufficient. I love to help others but find it extremely hard to let someone help me. I hate being dependent on others.

An Experience with an Angel

I was studying at the Franciscan Institute of St. Bonaventure University in New York when I had my first experience with an angel in 1974. The course of study for the six week session was very intense. The food service was excellent. There was a great deal of class time, research requirements that kept us in the library, and some time for recreation. My recreation was to be in the pool every day from one to two o'clock in the afternoon. Sometimes I would go with another friend. Many times I swam alone. There was usually a life guard on duty. Exercise was important to me because I had lost fifty-three pounds on a weight loss program and did not want to gain the weight back.

I do not consider myself to be an excellent swimmer. As long as I stay in relatively shallow water, I am okay. I do not dive. I do not do tricks. I tend to float a lot and exercise by doing multiple stretches and aerobics.

This particular afternoon I decided that my head was really stuffed with knowledge and I needed to just relax in the pool. I went with a friend and started my routine of trying to do a back stroke with intermittent floating. I was trying to relax. And indeed I did relax. Before I realized it, I had fallen asleep and woke up in twelve feet of water. I started to sink to the bottom of the pool. I tried to swim up to the surface, and when I thought I was close enough, I opened my mouth to scream "Help!" But all I could do was gurgle some sound and my mouth and lungs filled with water. The pain was excruciating, and I felt as if my chest was going to split right open. I sank even further down to the bottom of the pool. I tried a second time to reach the surface, did the same routine of trying to yell for help, and experienced even sharper pain and hopelessness. I knew I was going to die.

Then I was asked a question. "Have you been a loving person?" I could honestly say that I had tried to be. I wasn't perfect, but I had tried to be a loving person. Then there was a moment of truth. A voice inside my heart said, "What you learn with your head is not as important as what you learn with your heart." At that moment there came around me a strong presence of being embraced with divine love. It was the most peaceful moment I have ever experienced. All of a sudden my shoulder and arm were grabbed and slammed against the side of the pool. I was above water and breathing. I looked around to see who had helped me. My friend was at the other end of the pool, oblivious to what had happened. The lifeguard was no where around. I was saved, I believe, by an angel of God, who was sent to me to give me that very important message. This was my first experience of an angelic presence in my life and one that I will never forget.

Chapter Two

An Untimely Death

She was only fifty-eight years old, and I thought she would live forever. I was eighteen. It was a beautiful October day, and I was anticipating her coming home after a long hospital stay. I was told she had had a heart attack. One of my brothers had me convinced that I was the cause of her illness. I was an unreasonable teenager. I refused to believe that she was sick until she was taken to the hospital and kept there until she could be well again.

I went off to my college classes feeling a sense of joy that when I came home that evening, she would be there just like old times. But that never happened. Instead, I received a page in the middle of my class and went to a hallway phone. My brother told me to come to the hospital quickly. That was all he said. It didn't sound good.

I drove as quickly as I could. I ran up the steps to the floor where she was, entered the room, and saw a number of nurses and doctors around her. My Dad was an emotional wreck, banging his hand against his forehead and in tears. He took me over to the bed and told her, "Theresa is here." She opened her eyes and looked starry-eyed. She didn't recognize me. When I saw the blank look on her face, my heart was ripped away. I couldn't bear the thought that she didn't know who I was. I left the room quickly, shaking and in tears. My brother called after me, "Where the hell do you think you're going?" I didn't respond. I just kept running down the hallway, out to my car, and drove back to the college. When I finally got back to the parking lot, I saw the dean of students standing at the door. I knew that she was gone. I heard bells ringing and I knew. Mom was gone.

I drove back to the hospital and walked the stairs to the room I had visited just hours before. A nun wanted to take me into a conference room to let me know what had happened. I told her I already knew. I just wanted to see Mom. What was before a body with numerous tubes and hoses attached to it now was a beautiful, glowing woman. It was at that moment I knew for sure that there was more to this life than what we see. There is a resurrection life, and my mother was experiencing it. She looked at peace, and at that moment that peace radiated into my heart.

I was left with many unanswered questions that day. I was also very angry. I felt cheated and abandoned. I felt that all this was unfair. But I also felt that it is not good to question why God allows what God allows. So I stored all these feelings in my mind and heart. I added them to the baggage I would carry with me for the next forty years. Mom was gone and so was my childhood.

A Nighttime Visitor

It was about three o'clock in the morning when I was startled from my sleep. I woke up shaking and my heart racing. Then I sensed a presence in my room. It was almost as if there were a yellow-golden glow around me. I was scared and I prayed, "Lord, I don't know what you're doing, but I'm not into this kind of stuff. How 'bout you go visit someone else if that is who you are." Then I started to repeat, "Jesus is Lord. Jesus is Lord" until I could calm myself down. Then all was well. It was the night before a session I had scheduled with Doctor Cindy. We were going to do more energy work.

When I got up the next morning, I still had questions about what had happened during the early morning hours. I didn't think I wanted to share the experience of the golden presence because I really didn't want Doctor Cindy to think I was nuts.

I got into her office and we talked for a bit. Then she asked me what I wanted to address in our Reiki session. I told her that I was thinking a lot about my mom and how she died and why.

So that became the focus.

As I got onto the table, I wondered what this experience might be like. I can say that even although my mind was filled with lots of thoughts, not many that were making any sense to me.

We began the session with a prayer, asking Mary, the Mother of God, to be with us in a special way. She was asked to console us. The angels and saints were called upon to protect us and to be with us as we journeyed toward truth. And then we started our digging. We explored my relationship with my mom and her illnesses. We talked about what I believed my mother thought of me. I could recall the many situations where I did not feel supported by her. I could recall the criticisms about not doing the dishes well or ironing the clothes the right way, and how I was always looking for the easy way out of things. I was carrying all these mental tapes and playing them over and over. As I played them, my self-esteem continued to diminish.

Then we seemed to get to the real issues. We talked about her untimely death and how I felt abandoned. Then Doc said to me, "I want you to know that your mother is here and she is wearing a beautiful golden dress." At that point I experienced a flood of tears and I cried. I could tell my mother how bad I felt that she died when I needed her the most. I talked about the anger. I cried through the pain. And at the end of the session, as Doc held my head in her hands and stroked my forehead and cheek, I understood that mom's time was not her own. She had been called into God's time and it had nothing to do with anything I had done. Her death, when it happened, was to happen at that time for a reason. Sometimes we are just called to live with the mystery of those kinds of happenings.

The Picture

There is a picture of my mother that I have had for years. It is a very old picture that shows this Italian woman, hair in a bun, wearing a cardigan sweater over an old-fashioned dress. She does not seem to be smiling. It hangs in my office.

Every time I looked at this picture, I could feel my mother's disapproval. I could not see any love in the picture. I either found myself feeling guilty about something or feeling numb. But I kept the picture in sight.

After my experience with Doctor Cindy and the work we did on coming to some reconciliation with my mom, the picture took on a different look to me. I can almost see a smirk on mom's face. But it is a kind smirk. It is a look of "Hang in there, I believe in you."

Sometimes it is worth sorting through the muck of your life to find the treasure of a long, lost love that was always there. My mom loves me.

Chapter Three

The Need for Faith

I have often heard it said that we are our own worst enemy. I believe that's true. God's love, as told to us in the Scriptures, is constant and unconditional. There is nothing we can do that is so terrible that will make God turn his face from us. We do the turning. We do the rejecting. We experience the doubts and allow our faith to be shattered. We become afraid when we do not understand what is going on. We panic when we are not in control of the things going on around us. We experience the helplessness of our humanity when we can't find the answers to our life questions. Yet if we believe in God and God's love for us, we have the hope to hang on for one more moment, one more hour and one more day. We can try to convince our hearts that God is always there for us no matter the circumstances. This is what unconditional love is … a love that is forever, no strings attached.

This is where believing is important. Unless we believe in the tremendous love that God has for us, we can't fully enter into a God experience. If we don't believe in God's love, why would we believe that God loves us enough to send angelic assistance? It doesn't make sense. I think it's important to take time to explore the essence of our belief system. What do we really believe in? Perhaps it is more accurate to ask **who** we really believe in. Belief in God or a higher power, whatever name you want to give him or her, is essential. How do we get to that point in our spirituality?

11

Discovering Where God Is

I used to think I knew a lot about God. At one point in my early years, I thought I had God all figured out. Now I know I was nowhere near understanding God and what God expected of me. I carried a great deal of baggage with me whenever I tried to journey with God. My supply of Catholic guilt seemed never ending. Whenever I thought I was doing something right, I would start to question my intentions. Was I doing this good deed because I was a kind person? Was I doing it for the attention it would bring me? Was I trying to impress those around me? The questions continued to multiply until I would be so depressed and tired that I decided to remain frozen. I would choose not to act again. I continuously would twirl myself into a place of self-doubt. It was a lot of wasted energy. This was energy I couldn't afford to waste.

Chapter Four

Moving toward Understanding

It was important to me that I make some move toward understanding why food had become the prominent source of fulfillment to me. The more I thought about the place food had in my life, the more I could see that I was using it as a substitute for all sorts of things. When I was sad, I would eat. When I was frustrated, I would eat. When I was angry, I would eat. When I wanted to get together with friends, I would suggest breakfast or lunch. When at work, people were always celebrating events with food. Donuts, cookies, and many kinds of snacks were considered to be ordinary ways to let people know that something good had happened. And each time I participated in these festivities, I ate more than I needed to and then resorted to feeling bad. It was a senseless cycle that took hold of me and wouldn't let me go.

And the weight continued to change. It went higher and higher until I came to realize that the weight was starting to destroy the rest of me. It wasn't long that my knees started to hurt. My feet would swell. I was told I had lymphadema, an accumulation of water in my legs and ankles requiring me to undergo six weeks of treatment and the wearing of compression stockings for the rest of my life. I found out that I had developed Type 2 diabetes and soon was on insulin. Diet and exercise didn't help me control my disease. I developed high blood pressure. I could no longer go into a regular store and buy regular clothes. Catalogues for fat people became my daily mail. And soon I was diagnosed as depression. Who wouldn't be depressed? I now found myself being fat, sick, depressed, and taking medications for all of these illnesses. Every day I was required to pop twelve different medications into my body. I felt as if I was a walking pharmacy and I felt caught. I felt trapped in a body three times the size it needed to be. And I wanted to break out.

Faith and Therapy

So, I decided to see a pain doctor who tried to help people in chronic pain. The pain in my knees and back was unbearable. I underwent injection therapy on both knees and on my back, only to find that relief was very limited. I went from using one cane to two canes and having a hard time walking a long time or standing for more than a few moments. I could no longer walk reasonable distances anymore. Every thing seemed to be crashing in on me, and I felt desperate. Upon my pain doctor's recommendation, I went to see a therapist who helps people deal with pain. I found out that this therapist worked with obese people as well as those in chronic pain. The first meeting with her left me feeling unsure about what therapy was all about. She didn't seem to be the kind of therapist I could relate to. I didn't know what to say or how to say what I felt was wrong with me. I only knew that I was in pain and I didn't want to be in pain anymore. I wanted to break free.

Upon hearing me say this much, the therapist said to me, **"Do you know what you are asking for?"** At that point I wasn't sure what I was asking for. I only knew that I wasn't happy. I wasn't feeling good physically, and my soul felt as if it were dying a slow death. My emotions were tangled, and I knew that if anything good was going to come out of this doctor-patient relationship, I would need to trust. But, I was afraid. I had been hurt in relationships before, and I needed to think twice about taking a chance again. The doctor's words resounded in my head … **"Do you know what you are asking for?"** I needed to do some thinking about that.

Taking the Risk

I decided four weeks later to seek out the therapist's help in dealing with my obesity. She was welcoming, and I felt that we were in a good place to start unwrapping the bondage I was in. As we talked about why I had come back, I reiterated my statement about wanting to become free … free of the body fat that I was carrying and free of the ignorance I felt about allowing myself to get to this place. I knew that besides carrying so much weight around with me, I was carrying a lot of emotional baggage. This baggage had to do with what I had experienced during my life and how I had dealt with or ignored it. She looked at me and asked me to tell her about myself.

I didn't quite know where to start. I soon learned that any starting point is a good place to start. As I sat there sharing my early memories about home, how I was treated as a child, and how I felt about myself, I realized that I had a lot of work to do. I had a lot of baggage to unpack. This visit to a therapist was not going to be a quick fix for what I was experiencing. She would tell me nothing that wasn't already inside of me. I just had to face the demons within, dismiss them, and allow the grace of God to come live within me. Before I knew it, the second visit was over and I was on my way home, lost in questions and deep in thought.

I found it hard to go back to work and listen to people complain about the copy machine not working properly or messages not delivered in a timely fashion. Somehow I needed to process what was going on inside of me. I left the therapist's office with questions about how I felt about myself. I needed to trace back events in my life that had brought me to such a low opinion of myself. I couldn't help but ask the question, **"Why didn't I love myself?"**

The Third Visit

I didn't wait four weeks to make another appointment. I probably went back in two weeks, but during those two weeks I was finding myself doing a lot of praying and reflecting on how I was relating to myself. I found that I could be sensitive and caring to others. I could accept many of the shortcomings in others. But for some reason, I could never give myself the same breaks or compassion. I felt I needed to be perfect and I knew that I wasn't.

Those two weeks were very difficult for me. At first I felt like I wanted to go right back and see the doctor immediately. I had some things I wanted to say to her, butI wasn't quite sure what I wanted to say. I just wanted to be with her. I didn't want to sit with my thoughts. I was beginning to feel the pain of memories and I was afraid. She told me before I left her office that our focus for our next session would be to look at the feelings and events I could remember from the first five years of my childhood. The more time I spent trying to recall these years, the sadder I became. I felt very alone. But I couldn't put my finger on why I felt this way.

This next visit was pivotal in my growing in understanding. I felt very afraid to see the doctor this time. I was **very** afraid. When I got into the office, I sat there. She said to me, "Tell me everything." And I began to cry. No, it wasn't crying really. I sobbed. I didn't have any words. I just had the feeling that my heart was splitting open and pain was pouring out of me. I didn't say much at all. I let my body express the pain I was experiencing, and it did so in tears. She handed me tissue. **Lots of tissue.** Then, when I could manage to compose myself, I could tell her of an incident that occurred when I was five years old. It was an incident that obviously I had buried for fifty-three years deep in the core of me where no one could go.

Chapter Five

I Should Have Known Better

I am the youngest of nine children. My sister Nina is twenty years older than I am. When my Mom danced at my sister's wedding, she was pregnant with me. A year after my sister married, she gave birth to a son. My nephew Santo and I were very close in age and grew up together living in houses next to each other.

When I was five, I had a wonderful interest in model railroads. My nephew had a train set, and I loved watching them go around the towns and mountains and other scenes created by my brother-in-law. If you wanted my attention, all you needed to do was mention trains.

I was a very hard headed child. Sometimes I would listen and sometimes I didn't. I found it very hard to listen to my mother when she told me not to do something. It was as if her words went in one ear and out the other.

One day my mom was giving me a safety tip. She told me never to go through the alley way. In the alley, there was a house where one of my brother's friends lived. He was about 14 or 15. I was five. One day I was sent to the drugstore and I decided I would cut through the alley to save time. This boy was outside just hanging around. He asked me if I wanted to see his train set. Of course I did. And, of course, the train set was in the basement of his house. The basement door was one of those heavy doors that opened from the outside and needed to be pushed opened from the inside. There were steps leading to the basement.

When we were halfway down the steps, he asked if he could see my privates. I said no. Then he said he wouldn't hurt me. He just wanted to look. He attempted to try to pull my jeans down and I pleaded with him to leave me alone because I didn't think God would like it. As he tried to tell me God wouldn't care, I kicked him in the face, turned around quickly, pushed open the basement door, and ran as fast as I could down the block to my house. I ran in the back door and saw my three brothers sitting at the kitchen table. I was crying hysterically, and my mother asked me what was wrong. I told the whole story even though I knew I would get in trouble for disobeying my mother.

My brothers got up from the table. My one brother who was a friend of this boy said, "I'm going to kill the son of a bitch!" And off they went to beat the hell out of this guy. My mother held me. She didn't scold me. She let me cry. And as I was telling the story to the therapist, I realized that this is one of the few times I can remember feeling my mother's unconditional love and trust. It was also the beginning of my experience of being afraid of my own body and feeling a need to begin building a wall around myself.

Sexuality

I'm sure a lot happened in the next ten years that affected my attitude toward myself. My years in public grade school started with a love affair in kindergarten with a boy named Dennis. We were sure we would get married some day. We even bought each other penny candy when candy was still a "2 fer". For a dime you could come home with a bag full of "2 fers" …. two candies for a penny. And we often did just that.

During elementary school, I was always the fat girl. I remember my mom taking me to a clothing store and the clerk calling me a "chubby".

All my clothes came from the Chubby Department. What I couldn't understand was why clothes designers would call fat girls chubby and then design clothes made of lace and chiffon and embroidered flowers that would make us look even bigger than we were. Anyway, I was classified a chubby, and it did wonders for tearing my self-esteem apart. Besides that I was always called a "sack of potatoes" at home. This meant only one thing. All the other kids were tall and thin. I was just short and fat. And I ate too many fried potatoes.

This did wonders for my social awareness as well. Any time there was something going on at church, a dance or social, I would always be afraid that no one would talk to me or dance with me. I soon found out that boys don't like fat girls and skinny girls make fun of fat girls. They whisper behind your back and say very mean things. They exclude you from the playground conversations. Grade school was a very lonely experience for me.

It wasn't until high school that I thinned out a bit and found a group of friends that I could hang around with. We weren't the chicks that the jocks went after, but we had decent friends that we could talk to and dance with at high school or church dances. It was a time for fun.

Then sophomore year came and my parents told me that we were going to Sicily for six months. I would be taking all my textbooks with me and I would be expected to take midterms when we returned in October. We went by ship, and it was a very exciting experience until we arrived in the little village where my parents were born. They hadn't been home in thirty-eight years, and they were anxious to see relatives and friends they had left behind when coming to America. I didn't know what to expect. All I knew about Italy was what I saw in the movies. I expected that we would be living in a beautiful villa with green vines and grapes hanging all over.

My experience of being Sicilian was simple. My parents spoke only Sicilian in the house. I could understand it perfectly, but I could not speak the language that well. This made me a bit apprehensive about spending six months in this foreign land.

When we arrived in the village, I was shocked, to say the least. We had no villa. Instead, the living facilities were quite primitive. There was limited sleeping space and the kitchen served as a place to prepare and eat your meals. It also had a unique feature I had never seen: an indoor outhouse. It was a simple toilet surrounded by three wooden walls that did not go up to the ceiling. The hole in the toilet went directly into the ground three levels below. Every use of the toilet was followed by a bucket of water. There was always a stench, which limited the enjoyment one could have eating one's meals.

When we arrived at my cousin's house, I was told that because of limited sleeping space I would have a bed companion. My older female cousin who was twenty-two would be sleeping in the same bed with me. I hadn't ever slept with anyone, so this was a new experience. I was nervous about it. I didn't know what to expect from her. I just knew I felt uncomfortable. Six months seemed like it was going to be a very long time.

It wasn't more than a week after we were there that my cousin hit on me. Her advances caught me by surprise. I was sixteen and curious about what was going on within my own body. I knew that changes were taking place. Her touches frightened me, and although I tried at first to resist, I was told that she would go to my parents and tell them I instigated this activity. Contrary to all I had been taught about the sacredness of touch, I allowed this to continue in fear that my parents would think less of me if they knew of our sexual activities. I never felt good about this. Rather I feel extremely guilty that I was acting against the values I was taught. It was indeed a very long six months.

Guilty as Charged

When I realized we would be going home to America, I decided I should go to confession to the priest in a neighboring town. After all, what would happen to my soul if the plane crashed and I died? It was a challenge to try to put into Sicilian words what had happened and how I felt about it. When the priest asked me, "Are you engaged?" I knew that we were not on the same wave length. It seemed that Father was saying that the behavior I was engaging in would be appropriate if marriage was a future prospect. He obviously didn't understand that this was a lesbian experience confessed by a very confused teen.

I then decided to make a good act of contrition and hope that the airplane didn't crash on the way home. If it did, I just knew I would have a permanent reserved seat in hell. I also promised that when I arrived in the States, I would seek out an opportunity to go to confession to an English-speaking priest.

Confession Is Good for the Soul

Shortly after I arrived home, I found out that our parish was having a "Mission Week". This meant that there were visiting priests who would come and pray the Mass with us, give a talk, and give people the opportunity to go to confession. I stood in line with others waiting to pour out my sinfulness in hopes of receiving absolution and a ticket to heaven in the event death came.

Finally it was my turn to go into the box. I knelt down and stared at the screen in front of me. The priest was listening to the person on the other side of the box. When the priest would slide the door on my side, it would be my turn.

I wasn't sure what to say to the priest. When I was little, I would rehearse my list of sins. I disobeyed five times. I talked back to my parents twenty times. A laundry list is what we used to call it. But now this was a sexual thing. How in the heck do you tell a priest my female cousin hit on me in Italy and I didn't do anything about it?

The screen was slid back, and I started out with "Bless me, Father, for I have sinned … " I told him what happened and how I felt bad about feeling caught in a situation that I didn't feel I could do anything about. I expected him, this man of God, to reprimand me in some way for failing to have the courage to let the adults in my life know what was going on. Instead, he asked the most inappropriate, probing questions that confused me even more. For example, he asked me who of the two of us was more fully developed. Then he continued by asking who seemed to enjoy the sexual behavior more.

I was surprised at the questions and I became afraid. Then he said that he bet that I wouldn't have the courage to come to the rectory that afternoon and face him in person and ask for his blessing. I told him I would if I had to in order to be forgiven. My mind was swirling, and I was really in a state of mental chaos. I just wanted to make things right with God.

That afternoon I did go to the rectory. I was a sixteen-year-old-girl, afraid of going to hell, asking the priest I thought I could trust to give me a blessing. When I arrived at the rectory, Father met me at the door. He seemed surprised to see me and invited me into a parlor room. I sat in one chair and he sat in another across from me. He told me he was proud of me for coming to the rectory to be reconciled with God. He asked me to kneel for his blessing. I knelt on the carpeted floor at his feet. He extended his hands and rested them on my head. He gave me his blessing and then hugged me for what seemed to be an eternity.

As I walked home that afternoon, I was without any feeling at all. I did not feel relieved. I did not feel forgiven. I did feel betrayed. Later on, when I was older, I realized that this priest had spiritually and emotionally abused me. I think he was finding pleasure in my pain. And even though he did not sexually abuse me in a physical way, the damage he caused to my soul and psyche stayed with me for many, many years. It was another bout with abuse.

My Abused Heart and Soul

It wasn't until therapy that I realized in my first sixteen years of life I had experienced sexual abuse on three levels … the friend of the family, a relative ,and a trusted adult, a clergyman. In all three experiences, I now know my self-esteem had diminished if not altogether disappeared. I experienced a variety of feelings. I felt shame, guilt, and fear of God. I felt bad about decisions I had made and courage I did not exhibit. My intention was to make things right with God and to do whatever was required to have that happen. Instead, I was betrayed, and I felt more the abandonment of God than God's compassion. I was angry as well as I tried to deal with a number of feelings that I could not understand or resolve. So I packed them away. But one feeling that remained with me was that I would never let this happen to me again. I would do anything to prevent being in this kind of circumstance again. I would be in control.

Chapter Six

Building the Wall of Fat

I think I mentioned that I feel as if I have been fat my whole life. The layers that keep me protected from hurt didn't form overnight. The layers represent a variety of situations where I feel that I was rejected or looked down upon. I never knew self-confidence in high school. I never felt smart or pretty or popular. Even though I dated and "went steady", I never was part of the "in" crowd. I was just one of those ordinary kids who goes to class, comes home and does homework, and sits bored the rest of the night. Weekends were anything but exciting for me.

It wasn't until sophomore year of college that an art teacher believed in me and encouraged me to go into fine arts and teaching. I did okay in college, but I never felt like I could possibly go on in education. In fact, my first choice of level teaching was kindergarten to third grade because I felt I would at least be smarter than those little kids.

But soon I was introduced to the world of art and artistic expression. I found an outlet for all the feelings and sensitivities I was discovering were part of me. Jewelry-making gave me the opportunity to work in solitude with a media that required skill and patience. Graphic arts moved me to explore the world of color. My real love, however, was and is painting. Painting presents a blank white canvas and asks for feelings, ideas, and dreams.

Soon I discovered that I was meant to be an art educator. I never believed I was a good artist, but I grew into becoming a damn good teacher. I knew the struggles that a person without self-confidence must endure or overcome, especially when it comes to one's creativity. I struggled with many media. I flopped when it came to ceramics and trying to throw a pot on the pottery wheel. I'd made many creative ashtrays in my college years and I didn't even smoke! I learned the techniques—and in many situations how *not* to teach.

For example, I was often belittled by my ceramics teacher because I lacked skill in this area. Her lack of support made me feel inadequate. I experienced the hurt of these encounters, and as I continued studying art and education, I vowed never to hurt a student as I had been hurt. I grew into knowing how to recognize and encourage the gifts in others, but I was blinded to my own gifts.

Those were years when I knew I was afraid of what my future might be. I was afraid of relationships with both sexes. Although I dated in high school and in college, my experiences both with males and females made me very nervous. I didn't feel I could trust my feelings. I felt very needy, and although I did have friends, I never felt as if anyone really cared for me or loved me for who I was. I know now it was because I didn't care or love myself. I didn't know who I was, and what I did know about myself, I didn't like. For this reason I needed to protect myself from letting anyone get too close to me. I was lonely, but I couldn't afford to let my guard down. I didn't want to be hurt anymore.

So I looked for another kind of companionship. Food became my comfort. Food became my primary friend. Food became the major reason for my relating with other people. If we were eating, we didn't necessarily have to talk much, and if we did talk, we discussed the quality and quantity of what we were eating. We didn't have to be creative about how to spend our evenings or weekends. If there was nothing else to do, we could go hang out at a fast food restaurant.

And my body grew and grew.

I then decided I needed to do something about this weight gain. I went to see a general practitioner who prescribed diet pills. They made me extremely jumpy. Then I graduated to the famous weekly meetings, but I found those difficult to attend. I also tried grapefruit diets that gave me an acid stomach, eggs and high protein that raised my cholesterol, low fat diets, no-fat diets, and no-taste diets.I bought a membership to a gym. No, two gyms, I think. I bought a ski machine, a stationery bike, an ab machine, and a trampoline. I owned jump ropes, went skating, and even tried jogging. I had a bike and an assortment of weights for strength building.

I can remember how I felt when my jeans didn't feel quite right. They were uncomfortable and hard to zip and button. I solved that problem first by purchasing a bigger size and later by graduating into "women's" sizes. Most women's clothes have elastic waists. So it didn't seem to matter whether the weight increased. Pants came with enough elastic that stretched around my fat waist and thighs. As I continued to pack on the pounds, I had to move farther and farther up the size rack. Soon there were no more sizes left on the rack, and I had to resort to catalogue clothes.

There's Nothing Cool about Big Sizes

I don't care how one may try to state it: there is nothing cool about big sizes. Whether the store is named Sizemore, Big & Tall, Queen's Closet, Woman's World, Chubbyville, or Omar the Tent Maker, big clothes for big women are not as attractive as those for smaller sizes. They also cost more. I suppose it's because you need more material. Whatever the reason, if you are big, you need companies that make big clothes. You are at their mercy. Or you go around naked.

Catalogue shopping becomes expensive, too, because not only are you paying for the product and the shipping, but many times you need to pay additional shipping when you send the stuff back. So many things I thought looked good in a catalogue looked awful on me. Maybe it was because the models for these catalogues are the tall sizes, not the wide sizes.

Once I signed up for one catalogue, it seemed that every fat shop in the country was getting me on their mailing list. I continue to get three to four catalogues a week trying to entice me to buy their products because their styles will make me look thinner. But big is big and disgusting is disgusting and tight is tight. Clothes cannot camouflage the body. Clothes can make one look neat and presentable, but a person knows when she or he is overweight, and there is nothing attractive about that.

It came to a point where I could only order from catalogues, and I did that. Then I would wait for the packages to come. When they came, I would let them sit on the living room couch for a few days. I hated the fact that they were from a fat people's factory. After a few days the packages would be put in my room and when I had enough nerve, I would go into my room, open the packages and try things on. One by one I would realize that either the neckline was too large, the sleeves too long, or the midsection too tight. Some I could wear once and then had to return them because they would shrink after the first washing. Frustrated, I would gather things back up, make out the forms, and then send the stuff back. I often felt as if the whole world knew what I was returning. I could hear the world screaming, "Hey, Fatso, stuff doesn't fit. You must be getting bigger!" I went back to the solace of food even though it was food that was causing me such pain.

And my body grew and grew.

Chapter Seven

What Was Really Going On?

Facing the truth about myself led me to ask the question, **"What was really going on?"** You see, I don't believe I got to this point overnight. It took years of self-hatred, self-abuse, and self-denial to bring me to a place where I just couldn't care anymore. The hurts I experienced in my life time were buried deep inside the fat tissues. My therapist would often say, "Your issues are in your tissues." The lack of self-love, self-confidence, and self-fulfillment were locked away in a big, fat body. And I used this body to make myself present to the world. I may have not been able to control my eating, but I could say something with my size. No one could miss me. I was too big to be ignored. But I also felt the pain of the attention I was getting. And there was no glory in that. The stares I would receive hurt me deeply. Believe me, I got stares from lots of people.

One day I went shopping in a discount store. Because of my size and the pain in my arthritic knees, I had to use a motorized cart. I remember a little boy sitting in the seat of a regular cart saying to his mother, "Mama, look at the big grandma over there. She is really big." His mother turned his head and told him to be quiet. But I heard him, and his words hurt me. I realized the little boy was telling the truth. My giant size and gray hair did classify me as a really big grandma. I didn't enjoy shopping that day. I wanted to go and hide. I wished I was home, away from the stares of others. I wanted to run away from these people and myself.

I shared this encounter with the therapist the next time I saw her. She advised me to try to say a little prayer for any one who seemed to be staring at me or taking a second glance because of my size. So I tried that. Whenever my eyes met those of someone looking my direction, I would pray, "Lord, give them the gift of compassion. Try to help them see that I don't really want to be this way. I'm working on being better." It was a way of turning a moment of pain into a moment of grace, if not for that person, then for me. I prayed that prayer a lot. I still pray it today.

Many of my friends would talk about losing weight and how they could lose weight easily. That would hurt, and it made me envious of them, their metabolic systems, and their bodies. I watched others eat tons of snacks and food and remain thin. Anger would rise up in my gut. There were many who invited me to share a meal with them, and many times I felt compelled to in order to be part of the group. This made me feel weak and without determination to change my habits. I felt that I was expected to be the happy fat person, and many times I was just that. I would crack fat jokes and others would laugh. But at night, when I was alone, I knew that there was nothing funny about being obese. There was nothing funny about dealing with life-threatening diseases day after day. I soon came to the understanding that there was nothing funny about being fat.

Trying to Lose It

Don't misunderstand me. It's not that I didn't try losing weight. As I mentioned before, I tried a lot of methods. When I was in college, a doctor told me I had to lose weight and proceeded to give me diet pills. I lost weight, but I also nearly lost my mind. I couldn't concentrate in class nor could I sleep at night. I felt like a zombie, so I gave up the pills and went back to eating. Many, many programs and gizmos later, I still found myself to be extremely overweight and very unhealthy. I was only twenty years old.

When I went in for my annual physical, another doctor told me I better lose weight or I would die at an early age. So I decided to go to Overeaters Anonymous. We met in a church basement. I met someone by the name of Millie who took me under her wing. The room was crowded with lots of fat people who smoked and took turns blaming other people for their eating habits. Mother-in-laws, mothers, fathers, and spouses were the major cause for people overeating. Folks said they overate because they were bored, excited, lonesome, crabby, and on and on and on. They talked about following a 12-step program and shared where they were on their journey. I went to meetings for about six months but noticed little difference in my weight. I wasn't sure why I overate at that stage of my life. I just knew that I wasn't a very happy person. I didn't know what to do.

Then a group of my colleagues decided we would all go to weekly weight management meeting together. We pledged to eat lunch together so we could support each other. I wrote a simple and encouraging newspaper for just our little group, mentioning good recipes and complimenting others on their achievements in weight loss. For every quarter of a pound a person lost, she would receive a paper slab of butter. We used these paper symbols to build another person on the closet door of my art classroom. Only the members of our "fat club" knew it was there. Together the four of us created a 125-pound girl. Fifty-three of those pounds were contributed by me. I felt good about myself and liked how I looked. I can remember lying in bed one night and discovering that I could actually feel a rib where a rib is supposed to be. I remember how amazed I was.

Soon after that I was married and had children. The 180-pound body that I possessed soon disappeared. I grew and I grew. I tried numerous other diets. Atkins seemed to be a way to try to cut carbs. South Beach was popular with some of the people I worked with. Grapefruits, bananas, protein only, low-fat, no-fat, liquid diets … you name it, I think I tried it. I even tried listening to tapes and hypnosis. But to no avail. I couldn't get a handle on what was happening.

Then I found out I was diabetic, and even with that disease I couldn't get control over my eating. Diet and exercise were the continuous words I heard from any doctor I went to. My blood sugars were not under control. So I was put on oral medications. Then my blood pressure was high. So I was put on medication. My cholesterol was higher than the doctor wanted. So I was put on medication. Because of the weight gain, I was having some trouble with my bladder. So I was put on medication. Then I developed a knack for retaining water. So I was put on medication. And, finally, I was diagnosed with depression. And I was put on medication. All in all, every part of me seemed to be falling apart, and I could still not get control over my food. My body grew and grew. And I felt stuck.

A Recommended Solution

I wanted to find a new endocrinologist to help me with my diabetes. She was a woman doctor, very respected in her field. She said to me, shortly after coming into the room, "Have you ever considered gastric bypass surgery?" I was insulted. She touched the back of my neck and said to her assistant, "Make note of how much fat is back here." I didn't feel as if this doctor respected me. So when I left the office, I left her care.

I had an appointment with a cardiac physician's assistant. She was pleasant and supportive and I liked her a lot. We worked for a while trying to get my weight down. Then at one of my regularly scheduled check-ups, out of the blue, she said, "Have you ever considered gastric bypass?" I got mad. I wouldn't hear of it. I wasn't convinced that this new method of helping obese people was for me. Like I said, I got mad and didn't go back to see her for months.

I was having some difficulties with gynecological matters and so made an appointment for my exam. The doctor said it was very difficult to get the biopsy that he needed. He said, "I think you should consider gastric bypass surgery." I went home and cried.

My pain management doctor told me he couldn't do any more for me. I have arthritis in my knees and my lower back. My joints were not meant to cart around all of this weight. I should exercise more. He told me to take my life back or I would surely be unhappy for the rest of the time I had left. He advised me to look into gastric bypass surgery. Again I became angry and frustrated. I wanted to plug my ears so I wouldn't have to listen anymore.

And then there was my primary care physician. He looked at my chart and realized that I was beyond weight that he could measure on the scale. With his compassionate eyes he gently said he felt sorry for me. He knew that I always sat on the examining table because I did not fit in the chair. He understood that it was hard for me to walk. He knew it was embarrassing to be a younger person and have to use a cane or walker. He realized that I had tried to lose weight in the past. Then he gently said to me, "Please don't take this the wrong way. Have you ever considered what gastric bypass surgery could do for you? It could change your life." His was the first voice I heard and trusted. Yet he frightened me. He frightened me enough that I went into therapy where I could begin dealing with the bigger questions and bigger issues I knew were within me.

Chapter Eight

Unpacking the Baggage

I knew that my work with emotional baggage was just beginning. Doc, the affectionate name I call my therapist, challenged me to begin unpacking the experiences that were causing me pain and self-hatred. We needed to talk things out so that I could understand the **why**. In searching out the "why" I overate, I felt as if I hit a wall. I had no control or discipline left in me. I believe the depression over being so obese had left me numb. I was carrying four hundred pounds of body weight wherever I went. Deep in my heart I knew this would never get better unless I considered surgery. Doc told me to think about gastric bypass surgery. She told me it could change my life.

I got pissed at her. I was so angry, I decided to screw it. I would just take my chances … live as long as I was meant to live and then die. I didn't care anymore. I wasn't going to let her tell me that I should be letting someone cut up my insides and tell me what I could and couldn't eat. In no uncertain terms, I told Doc that if she ever mentioned this surgery again to me, I would not come back to therapy. I put her in her place.

Our sessions weren't the same. I felt I had put the kibosh on what could happen in our sessions. Doc had the courage to say to me, "If you don't have the surgery, you won't make it. You have too much to give to this world. Do you really want to die?"

At that point in my journey, I did. I did want to die. I couldn't stand myself anymore. I couldn't look in a mirror. Every time I did look at myself, it was with contempt. I continued to wear clothes that would cover my sin of not caring for myself. I felt guilty about letting myself get so big. I felt as if I had failed myself. I did not want to live. I did not want to explore any more feelings or behaviors. I wasn't sure what I wanted. The pain was so great I wanted to hide.

But Doc hung in there with me, posing the questions she felt I needed to hear and pushing me to the place where I would deal with the denial and walk through the pain of my past and present. She encouraged me to trust that God had a light at the end of the tunnel for me. I just needed to walk and work through this mess of what was being called life. I would come out the winner. I left her office that day with some serious thinking to do.

After filtering through much of the initial emotions of that session and coming to the reality that I did have to make a decision, I found myself withdrawing into my own world. I felt troubled and had a tough time concentrating on my work. I was a pastoral team member specializing in working with children and parents. I found myself unable to listen and unable to care about anyone else. I was so introspective at this point that the rest of the world didn't matter to me.

The more I thought about the possibility of surgery, the more afraid I became. I was convinced that at four hundred pounds, undergoing such a procedure would surely be the death of me. There was a battle going on inside me. I would move from wanting to die to being afraid to die. I felt caught in a whirlwind of confusion and fear.

I looked for excuses why the surgery would not work for me. Money was the primary reason. I had no idea if my insurance would pay for such a surgery, and if it didn't, then the decision would be made for me. I simply could not afford to self pay or time pay. If the insurance refused to cover it, I would simply take it as a sign from God that it was not meant to be.

I began to pursue gaining information about what my insurance covered. I was hoping that they wouldn't cover anything. I could never afford a $25,000 to $30,000 procedure and hospital care. That was a way of turning from the surgery. Then I found out that before the insurance company would permit surgery, I had to find a reputable program and surgeon. I had to have my primary doctor document six months of care concerning weight issues, which included a weigh-in each month. I also had to have a psychological evaluation submitted in writing. Then, and only then, would the insurance company consider allowing me to have this surgical procedure, paying most of the cost as covered in our benefits plan.

I called on the angels, especially Michael and Raphael, to help me in this decision-making process. I needed Michael to protect me from myself. I needed him to show me that fear never accomplishes anything and that fear is the primary weapon the evil one uses to keep us from being the best we can be for God. I needed Raphael to be my healer and companion. In the Bible Raphael often accompanied people who were searching for truth. I needed to face my fears and embrace the truth that God just might want me to have this procedure to help myself.

I prayed like I never prayed before. As I prayed and placed all my fears and hopes before God, I was filled with many thoughts. I thought about my children. I felt they needed me to be around for a while. I thought about wanting to see my children's children when the time came. I also wanted to grow old with my husband. I wanted to have retirement to look forward to. I wanted us to experience the freedom to enjoy each other's company after working so hard all our lives.

And so, together with the angels, my family, Doc, and five other doctors that I was seeing on a regular basis, I decided to go forward with the process and let myself be transformed from a person doomed to die to a person moving toward life.

Initial Meeting with the Bariatric Team

It took a lot of courage for me to walk into the conference room. I made the initial phone contact and registered for the information meeting. It was to be almost three hours long. When I walked into the room with my walker, I felt embarrassed to be there. I felt as if I was the heaviest person in the room. I noticed the chairs were much wider than the normal armchairs that I often had to cram my butt into. There was water out for those who wished. I sat with my can of Diet Pepsi. Handbooks and folders were given out with the information one needs in considering this surgery.

Members of the team came in one by one to speak to us. There was a finance and insurance person. There was a dietician who explained the change in foods that would be necessary. There was a nurse who explained the pre-surgical procedures as well as the post-surgical demands of this surgery. There would be specific dietary guidelines for me to follow before surgery to decrease the size of my liver and after surgery to accommodate the new digestive process. My stomach would no longer be the size of a normal adult's stomach. Instead, a small pouch holding approximately one ounce would be my primary source of intake of food. I would also be required to drink at least sixty-four ounces of water a day. Together with a gradual progression of various food textures, especially protein, the weight would come off. Abusing the pouch by eating too much or the wrong kinds of food could result in frequent trips to the bathroom or vomiting.

Then the surgeon spoke. I did not think he was a very likeable person. He minced no words. He told us what the surgery involved and how we would have to change our lives and eating habits if we wanted to be successful. He seemed like a real hard nose. He said numerous times that this surgery was not a quick fix but a tool to help a person lose weight and keep it off. But it was a tool we had to take and use. The work was ours to do.

I remember leaving that meeting with my husband and having him say to me, "That is really quite a commitment. I couldn't do that." And I remember thinking that I didn't think I could do it either.

When I returned to see Doc, I shared with her that I heard all the information but I didn't think I could do it. It was too drastic a change for me. She told me that she would walk with me all along the journey in this. I told her I was afraid that I would die on the table. She assured me that could be a possibility, but she didn't think so. She felt God had too much for me to do yet.

With her encouragement and my depending on the angels, I decided to move forward. I knew it would take six months to document my weight treatment with my primary physician. I believed that in that time I would be led to either a yes to the process or decide not to go through with it. Meanwhile, during this time I would continue meeting with Doc and offering this journey to God. I knew I had lots of issues because I was carrying lots of tissue.

Chapter Nine

No Scale Could Hold Me

It's one thing to be fat, or should I say morbidly obese. It's quite another to realize that there are certain consequences one pays for being this way. I can't count the number of times I felt humiliated when I tried to sit in a chair in the doctor's office waiting room only to find that my butt was bigger than the chair could hold. I tried to sit sideways hoping no one would notice. Then, when walking became so difficult, I found myself clinging to a wheel chair, a big one of course. Once I found a chair that would accommodate my huge body, I stayed in it. I had to depend on other people pushing me from place to place because walking was so difficult. I gradually lost my independence.

I became aware of the difficult road I was beginning when I realized I had to meet with my doctor for six consecutive months. I was supposed to be weighed each month, and I would need to meet with a dietician. The doctor asked me if I knew what I weighed. I told him about four hundred pounds. There wasn't a scale in his office that would weigh anyone over 350 pounds. So I asked the doctor to please document that truth … I was too much to weigh each month. He said he would and that's exactly what he did. I found him and his staff to be very supportive of what I was preparing for. I could feel the compassion in my primary doctor's voice. He was very aware of my struggles and he was very kind. He even apologized every time he had to write an order for a test concerning my obesity. He had to state the situation. He did. I was morbidly obese.

During the six months of waiting, a great deal of thought process was going on inside of me. I was so afraid of the surgery that I cried often. The most I could tell anyone is that it had been recommended by five of the physicians I was seeing for various problems. The common culprit in all of my troubles was the weight. It was a clear truth that stared me in the face everyday as I took insulin four times a day and swallowed twelve different medications every day. I couldn't wait until the six months were over. Even though I was afraid of dying, I knew that I was no longer living. I was in a whirlpool of fear and depression that was tearing me apart inside.

I continued to meet with Doc trying to work things through. She was a great help in keeping me on track. Doc helped me to see that fear was "false evidence appearing real". I had to work on not being afraid. I had to work on trusting God, myself, my doctors, and her. I realized I was being asked to trust them all with my life. I was scared. I felt that a lot was being asked of me. I wasn't sure exactly why I had such a fear of death. All I knew for sure was that I wasn't very happy and that life was not as good as I heard it could be.

Rejected

I was shocked the day the letter from the insurance company came. My request for gastric bypass surgery was considered unnecessary. How could this happen? I didn't understand the decision at all. I was coming closer to taking the step toward surgery, and the insurance company was pushing me aside. This was not the end of the battle by any means. Now I was more determined than ever to have that surgery. They would not refuse me. I would do what I needed to do to be able to make the choice of whether to have the surgery or not.

The battle was beginning. The bariatric staff submitted more medical records. The fact that I was diabetic and had hypertension, high cholesterol, depression, bladder control difficulties, and arthritis in both knees and back apparently didn't make a difference to the insurance company. But they were not living in this body of mine. The staff resubmitted paperwork along with recommendations from my other physicians, and by the end of November I received another letter affirming that the cost of surgery and care would be covered in full.

I felt that God had given me a clear sign that this was a gift of new life. New possibilities seemed to be right in front of me. All I needed to do was to take the step toward new life. The journey started in June and turned a corner in November. I turned a corner, too, in my attitude and determination to take my life back. With God and the angels, my husband and family, my best friend and many other supporters, and a great medical team, I would have another chance at life. I met with the surgeon and the date for surgery was set at March 20. It seemed a long time to wait, but I started to see all of this in God's time.

God's Time

God's time is God's time. There is nothing I can do to change God's time. Now that I felt eager to have the surgery, I was being called to wait. I am not a very patient person. When I want something, I want it now. But God knew I wasn't ready to start a new life. That's what this surgery was demanding of me. Nothing would be the same again. There were certain eating habits that I needed to change. There were still issues that I needed to deal with. I needed time even though I didn't think I did. God knew that I did. And when I mentioned this to Doc, she, too, believed that everything would work out as intended.

Who's in Control?

Sometimes I think I know everything. There are times when I know a great deal about a particular subject or topic. I am a control freak. I like to have things develop the way I think they should. I am happiest when I feel I can direct the life I live. When situations come up that I have no control over, I become very agitated. I search and search within myself for ways to make things come out the way I want them to.

I learned a great deal at this point of my journey. I learned that I would have no control over when and how all this would develop. I was being asked to trust. I was being asked to trust in a God I knew from my childhood and into adulthood … a God who loves me and wants the best for me. I was being asked to allow this God to guide me, hold me, secure me in love and wisdom. I was being asked to let go of all control and to submit to the will of a God who promises me unconditional love. What I had control over, I could govern. What I did not have control over, I would need to hand over and trust.

Chapter Ten

Surgery

I can remember how afraid I was the morning of surgery. My husband and my best friend took me to the hospital. I can remember having to go to the bathroom so many times I stopped counting. I remember the IV that they started me on and I remember going into the operating room. The room was cold, and everyone seemed so busy strapping this or that to me. I remember praying the Act of Contrition asking forgiveness for all I may have done to offend God or others in my life. As I was silently praying the Our Father, the anesthesiologist said he needed to insert a something or other down my throat so he could monitor my breathing. That process, whatever it was, was the most painful part of the surgery for me. Although I was semi-conscious for that part, I could feel myself resisting this foreign object in my throat. Then I gave it all over to God. And I was out like a light.

Recovery

I really can't remember anything about coming out of the surgery. I don't remember any of the pain. I take it for granted that they were giving me pain medication, but I have no recollection of it. One thought I have now, as I reflect on the events of that day, is that it was much like giving birth. When I gave birth to both of my children, I remember that I was in pain. But I can't recall a thing about the intensity of the pain because the joy of the outcome was overwhelming. Seeing a new life in my arms made it all worthwhile. And maybe, just maybe, that's what happened with this surgery. In a very mystical way I was giving birth to myself. I was claiming a new life, a new hope. I was soon to find out that the road ahead of me was nothing I imagined it would be.

The First Few Days

I had the surgery on a Tuesday, and by Thursday I was getting ready to go home. I tried eating the pureed food that the hospital provided. I tried. I could write a lot about how awful the food was and how just the thought of it made me sick. I was told the rules over and over. I was told to eat protein … pureed foods … water … drink, drink, drink. The nurses were constantly putting ice chips and water in front of me. They wanted me up and moving. I just wanted to stay in bed. If I couldn't stay in bed, I wanted to go home and be in my own safe place so I could feel free. I hated being watched and monitored. I just hated it.

Finally I was able to go home. I started trying to do what I had been told. Pureed tuna and chicken looked so unappealing. And I hated to drink water. I found it still difficult to move, and I got tired of the huffing and puffing that came with walking. What had I done? I had given up the love of my life—food. I began to question the wisdom of my decision.

By Saturday of that same week, I felt awful. It was hard to breathe. My best friend told me that she could hear me wheezing and told me to call the doctor or she would do it. When I called, I was told to come to the office on Monday morning. Ten minutes into the appointment, I was admitted to the hospital. I had pneumonia … and I was on the verge of dehydration. No one spoke about how long I was going to be there. All I heard was that I was a pretty sick puppy.

Fighting

It's hard to remember all the different technicians, therapists, nurses, doctors, student doctors, interns, and aides who came in and out of my room during the next eight or so days. One was telling me to breathe, one was telling me about the x-rays I would be having done, another was telling me to get up and walk, another was making sure that there was always water on my tray. I had more IVs in me than I care to remember. There was someone constantly coming in to draw blood. My veins were collapsing, and so the IV team was forever coming into my room to set up new lines. I really did feel like a pin cushion.

When it was time to eat, my tray came with pureed food on it and that was it. Pureed eggs have to be the most disgusting thing I've ever seen. I was ready to kill. I was angry and frustrated and I just wanted to die. And besides all of that, I had a pain in my chest every time I took a deep breath. I knew I was sick, but I was beginning to feel as if the cure was going to be worse than the disease.

Depression

It wasn't long before I realized that I was really over the edge. I was depressed. The eating wasn't getting any better and although I really gave it a chance, I just couldn't. I can't remember ever feeling as sick as I did during those days. Friends would come to visit me and encourage me to walk. One Sunday afternoon I ventured to do a walk in the hallway with my walker. I could barely get down the hall. There was a bulletin board in the middle of the hallway. It was filled with the pets of the nurses and aides on the floor and I was determined to walk that far and then rest. I got as far as the bulletin board, huffing and puffing as usual. I sat down on the seat of my walker.

As I was sitting there a little black child came out of his grandma's room, looked at me and said, "Lady, you sure is fat! I smiled at him and said, "I know, honey, but I won't be like this forever." Then I started to cry within. I was embarrassed and angry, and at that moment I decided that

I would not go walking in the hallways anymore. Of course, this made the doctor angry, but at that point I didn't really care. I wasn't going to be humiliated anymore. I had had it with people, and I found it very hard to understand why I was being subjected to this kind of abuse from the public. It was difficult to give myself a chance to change when it seemed others were so quick to judge.

In my head I could rationalize that it was the ignorance of people that causes obese people a great deal of pain. Unless you have walked in the shoes of a fat person who has tried everything to lose weight, you cannot understand the pain that this causes. Unless you have been laughed at out loud or stared at with smirks and looks of disgust, I think it is hard to really empathize with someone who is in the midst of this situation. The world is a cruel place for obese people to live in. Depression—giving up on yourself and being angry at the world—doesn't help the situation get better. But I just wasn't getting it. I carried a lot of anger within. I was angry at God. I was angry at people. But most of all I was angry at myself for not having taken better care of myself all these years. Now I was paying the piper for not doing so.

Home Again

I thought I would be happy to be home again. At first I was. I forced myself to eat pureed food and I even handled drinking more water than usual. I had an appointment with the physician's assistant, and she told me that I seemed to be doing fine. She suggested that I could try to eat a piece of toast and cheese if I cared to. I cared to.

Somehow I translated her words into a grilled cheese sandwich. Was this just wishful thinking? More like deliberate stupidity. I made my sandwich like I always did, with margarine and processed cheese, and sat down to eat it. I ate about a fourth of it, was full, and decided to take a nap. I woke up about an hour later in intense pain. The sandwich didn't stay where it was supposed to stay. After emptying the contents of my stomach pouch, I developed dry heaves, which caused violent pain to my ribs and abdomen. I thought a little water might help. It was a wrong move. For over twenty four hours I could not eat or drink anything. Whatever I tried immediately came out.

I called the doctor's office and was told to come in immediately. Ten minutes after arriving, I was admitted to the hospital again. This time I was put on IV' to build up fluids. I had nothing to eat for five days. I think this was an attempt to calm my stomach down. Finally, more tests were given to me only to discover that part of the opening for my digestive system was a bit too narrow. I heard them call it a "stricture". I underwent a procedure that would stretch the opening, much like angioplasty for the heart. A feeding tube was also inserted so that I could take some high-protein nourishment. About ten days later I was sent home with this appendage hanging off my left side. I had no idea what the next three weeks were going to be like.

People Coming and Going

There was a flurry of activity as I arrived home. I was now considered homebound. The physical therapist would come two days a week to help me walk and exercise. The occupational therapist would come two days a week. The visiting nurse would come three to four times a week. The man who was to teach me how to use the feeding machine came once a week for a number of weeks. The feeding machine required fourteen hours of down time. The feeding tube that was inserted on my left side was matched to a pumping machine that would gradually run vanilla-flavored protein drink into my body. The apparatus was clumsy and bothersome.

I had absolutely no social life during these weeks of feeding, but it was the only way to sustain my body while I could not take nourishment by mouth. It seemed as if every part of me was being overhauled at the same time. I continued to wonder when my life would be my own again.

Another Bout with Depression

I find it difficult to think about how depressed I was during the first weeks after the surgery. I was a mess inside. Everything was in the midst of change, and I had very little hope in the future. At this point I felt that I had made the biggest mistake of my life. When I spoke with the doctor, he simply said that he questioned if I had been ready for the surgery when I had it. I resented him for that. Actually, I resented him for a lot of things he said to me. In my eyes I felt that he was just a hard nose who never smiled. I did not care for his bedside manner. We seemed to be at odds with each other all the time. He felt I was being uncooperative when it came to the program. He told me that if I didn't get it together, I would surely die of starvation. Is that what I wanted?

I felt sad for a number of days. I mean, really sad. And then I decided to look at what I had forgotten to do … I had forgotten to try to place everything in God's hands. I had failed to ask the angels to help me pray. I was on such an independence kick that I didn't think I needed anyone. So I went back to Michael and Raphael and asked them to intercede for me and to help me to pray for what I needed at this point in my life.

The more I thought about it, the more I realized that I couldn't do it alone anymore. I needed to open myself to God. But God felt so absent from me. Even though I am in the religion business, I was weak in my faith in His love for me. In a humble spirit I turned to God and the angels and asked them to help me offer myself to God. I asked for the grace to allow myself to be helped by others. I asked for the wisdom to allow God and God's spirit to control my life. I asked for the courage to understand what was being asked of me. When I could lay all my frustrations, anger, and anxieties at the feet of the Lord, something wonderful happened that has changed my life, I think, forever.

Chapter Eleven

Recognizing the Loss

My weeks of recuperation were opportunities to do a lot of soul searching. However, instead of soul searching, I spent a lot of my time with pent-up anger. I played a lot of video games. I slept a lot. I felt sorry for myself. In the back of my head I kept hearing the doctor asking me if I wanted to die.

Through the grace of God, I remembered why I had set out on this journey to begin with. I wanted to see my children's children. I knew that could never happen if I didn't do something about my weight. That truth crept back into my head and my eyes seemed to be opened. I started to see the gifts around me and within me. For the first time in a long, long time, I felt myself realizing that I had gifts to offer this world and I was not about to leave the world without using them.

I prayed harder than I ever prayed. I prayed to be open to all the possibilities around me. I prayed to be able to recognize God present in my life again. I prayed constantly, asking the angels Michael and Raphael to take my prayers directly to the throne of God. I cried. And when I thought I was all cried out, I would cry more. I was coming to realize that something new was happening inside of me.

When something new happens, something else must die. In saying hello to one thing, I was called to say goodbye to another. I realized that

God was speaking to me through my family. My husband Jerry was one of my greatest supporters. He had to do many things that most men would have refused to do. The washing, cleaning, and cooking for himself were among the many tasks he had to take on. At the weight I was before surgery, there was very little I could do. It was an effort to walk, to carry anything, or to even stand at the sink to do dishes. All of these things that I did when we were first married he had to assume because I was too big to move. If marriage was for better or for worse, in sickness and in health, this seemed to be the ultimate test of our love. And I know, without a doubt, that he loves me. He has walked with me through every step of this process without complaint and with a hope that I could regain my health. For this I will be forever grateful.

My children knew I had made a very important decision, but I'm not sure if they understood the significant changes this surgery would have on my lifestyle. I could feel the support and see the patience they had with me as I no longer was cooking the way I did before. Even though my son Tony was twenty-three and my daughter Therese was nineteen, I could see that much of what I was going through was painful for them to watch. They still had their junk food to eat and enjoy but not without wondering how I could say no to such foods for the sake of my wanting to be healthy again. But they are thin and I was not. I could only hope that they would continue to learn from me the necessity to take care of one's health and well-being.

I realized that God was speaking to me through my friends who cared for me and picked up the slack at work for me. My best friend was and is always there for me without complaint about how time-consuming taking care of another person might be. I am cherished by many and especially my best friend who refused to let me think of dying. I was more conscious of how many people cared for me from my church community. They were praying for me daily. My pastor, too, gave me the time I needed to heal and become whole again. God was indeed speaking to me through many means.

The primary revelation I received was that I was grieving with both my heart and body. I had lost a good friend and that friend was food. I would never need to give food the power it had over me. I would never have a life that revolved around food. I would never be able to use food as a reason to be with friends. I would need to allow others to choose their foods and not feel like I was being denied mine.

I came to the understanding that everything in my life would be different and that all decisions are a trade off. I would be saying no to some things in order to say yes to the divine presence and will within me. Once I allowed myself to grieve, I could open my heart to healing. I needed to get rid of the hurt, frustration, anger, and junk that were clogging my heart so that I could ask to be filled with God's Holy Spirit. My angels helped me to do that. I was always asking them to help me feel so that I could heal.

Even the Doctor Noticed the Change

Even the doctor noticed the change in me. At my first follow-up check-in, he commented that my attitude was different. He told me he felt that I was ready to work with him and the program. And I was. I made a commitment to follow the rules. I would eat my pureed food. I would get the required amount of protein in every day. I would drink my water. I would exercise. Because I wanted to live, I would do whatever I was told. I needed to trust that the doctor and his assistants really were concerned about me.

One thought that kept me going throughout all of this was a truth that Doc told me: "This is not the way it will be forever." What enlightenment! I needed to eat this way NOW but not forever. This, too, would change as I grew in understanding how my new digestive system operated. I would gradually move onto to other foods as I could tolerate them. There was a light at the end of the tunnel that I felt I was in. I just couldn't see it until now.

New Attitude, New Energy

I had turned the corner. With my new attitude I found myself having more positive thoughts. I reflected a great deal on how I was changing. My new eating habits helped me to control my diabetes. I was taking four shots of insulin a day. My body required 128 units of insulin a day. I soon progressed to a point where I only needed one or two shots for a total of 21 units a day. I felt good about myself. I was becoming healthier and this was a small proof of that.

My energy level increased significantly. I found myself wanting to do more. Sitting around was not as satisfying as it used to be. I knew that I needed to get involved in some sort of exercise. I pictured myself being able to dance again. But I knew that all that would not happen all at one time. It was going to be a slow road back from the immobility that I had. I found myself feeling better when I wasn't spending time harboring bad thoughts or frustrations. I was constantly asking for heavenly help and I received it.

Creativity

I am an artist by degree. I have lots of media that I use to express my inner self. What I once had—the excitement about creating images to express my inner journey—returned. I continued to be able to share these images and works with others. I spent time and energy praying as I worked, experiencing the great joy that an artist has when an inner thought or idea is brought to birth. It is hard to put into words the rush I receive when I finally settle myself into creating. It is as if the hand of God is holding the brush, ripping the paper, singing the song, or drawing the image through and with me. What a marvelous gift to be given.

Changes in Social Interaction

One of the greatest challenges I have had to face is that of social interaction. There were very few occasions that I would gather with friends or family that did not involve food of some type. Whether it was going for a quick fast food lunch or out to dinner at a fancy restaurant, food was the center of my life. Buffets were my favorite because I could eat as much as I wanted in order to get my money's worth. Even though I would feel stuffed and uncomfortable at the end of the meal, it didn't matter. They would make no money off of me. I got my money's worth. Many times I didn't even taste the food. It was acceptable to eat fast, digest poorly, and sit for hours munching and being with friends. The biggest topic discussed was very often the quality of the food.

That changed. I became lost as I could no longer call someone up and say, "How about getting together for lunch?" Very few restaurants cater to gastric bypass patients. The foods I could eat, I couldn't get in a restaurant with the surety of having it prepared in a manner acceptable to my digestive system. It was important for me to avoid foods made with butter. Fried foods were out of the question, as were red meats and salads. Excessive sugar could cause violent stomach cramps and vomiting without warning. Portion control was extremely important. A normal restaurant meal equaled four portions for my newly constructed digestive system.

So for a long time we saved a great deal of money because I didn't eat out.

I had to search out other ways to invite friends to get together. I did. The focus just had to be different than food. Many of my friends and co-workers wondered how I could be so strong in resisting the temptations of sweets. But I wasn't strong. I was afraid that if I ate something that I was told wouldn't agree with me, it would make me sick. I don't particularly care to feel sick, so I listened to what I was told. I found myself experiencing more discipline than I have ever experienced. My strength came from God. My strength came from the guardian angels that would help me to do what I needed to do.

Changes Happen and the Challenge Is to Think Thin

Soon I began to experience changes, both physically and mentally. I was losing weight and I was dropping sizes. My clothes were getting bigger on me, a feeling I hadn't experienced in a long, long time. In fact, when I had surgery, I was in the biggest size the catalogue carried. They had no jeans that would fit me. I resorted to wearing big men clothes, and even they were difficult to handle. I did not feel very feminine anymore. I felt like I should have my clothes made by Omar the Tentmaker.

But, now my body was changing. What was solid fat on me was becoming jiggly. I could hear the flaps of skin hitting against my upper thighs, but not as loudly as I did before surgery. My body was changing, and I could feel the internal action of fat leaving me. The more protein I ate and the more water I drank, the more I felt my body readjusting.

It isn't enough to have the body change. It's important to start thinking thin. Yes, I knew I had about two hundred pounds to lose, but I was closer to that goal than I was before surgery. I knew that people still looked at me and wondered why I was so fat, but I knew that I was thinner than I used to be. I believe the evil one uses all of these demeaning tricks to discourage us from our journey. I needed to stand firm in my resolve that I would be healthy again. I couldn't care that much about what others thought. They didn't know the old me, so they couldn't appreciate the changes going on in me. I would pray for those who gave me looks or laughed at me. I heard the comments of children and their parents. But I tried very hard not to let these things disturb my inner sense of peace. I had to approach them with compassion even though they might not be able to be compassionate toward me. There was a new attitude developing in my heart.

Illnesses can teach us a great deal. My illnesses helped me to focus on what is really essential in life. Keeping a grudge, being impatient with others, trying to micro manage every activity, or allowing others to take away my joy is a waste of time. I try to remember that God wants me to be happy. I am learning every day that I want to be happy. I feel as if my priorities are pulling together and I can see clearly now. Love is of the essence. To walk in love is not just a sappy phrase … it is the truth. When I walk in love, I am so much happier than when I don't allow the truth to penetrate my life.

The Progression

One of the most interesting experiences for me was how my new digestive system needed to grow in accepting food just as my spiritual self needed to grow in accepting the divine presence within. There are certain disciplines that one who undergoes gastric bypass surgery must adhere to in order to reach success. The degree of success depends on the choices one makes.

You begin with pureed food, and, when well tolerated, you advance to soft foods. When your system can handle that level of food, you advance to another level. To move too quickly is to choose disaster. There is always the possibility of injuring your pouch by eating foods that are too rough for the newly developed system. It takes time and patience. But because I was in awe of the mechanics of this new tool for weight management, I started to see the weigh loss happen. The enemy was always the scale, the monster that would judge my success or failure. Now I realized that the scale was not a threat to me anymore. I actually started to look forward to my monthly weigh ins because it was an affirmation of the hard work I was putting into getting my life back together. I was working hard and this was a visible sign of that.

Another truth that I discovered about myself was that the numbers didn't matter anymore. I was doing something, and because I was doing something about regaining my health, I felt good about myself. These positive feelings about myself created energy within. As I saw the pounds come off, I could do a number of things without the huffing and puffing that I found so discouraging. I was at a turning point. Life was becoming more and more interesting every day. I looked forward to getting up in the morning and was happy to go to bed at night. My outlook on life is more positive, and I am challenged every day to try to do something that I couldn't do before at four hundred pounds. This was the beginning of a whole new adventure in living.

Chapter Twelve

Investing in Myself

For many years, everyone else came first. As a child, I wanted to please my parents. As a teen, I wanted to please my friends. As a teacher, I wanted to please my boss. As a wife, I wanted to please my husband. As a mother, I wanted to have the respect of my children. I was always taught not to place myself first because that was being selfish. So I didn't place myself first. Many times the things I wanted to do were put on the back burner so that other things could be done. I wanted to be the loyal friend, the good employee, the dutiful wife, the cool mother. I wanted to be what everybody else thought I should be. But, I wasn't me. I devalued myself because of the needs of all the other people in my life.

Gastric bypass surgery almost forces a person to invest in herself. In order for the surgery to be successful, one must focus inward and pay close attention to what is going on. If this tool is going to work, I know I have to put myself first. I must make choices not only in food but in activities that are life-giving for me. I have to choose to be good to myself.

It isn't easy. When you spend so many years telling yourself that everyone else is important and you are the least important, it is difficult to do a turn around. I keep remembering the words my husband uses when I am concerned about this or that, especially with the cost of things: "You're worth it." Why is it so hard for me to see and believe that? I take courage in his words and day by day try to believe that I am worth it ... .whether it is buying new clothes that fit or foods that I should be eating. I am worth it. The better I become for myself, the better I will be for others.

A Move toward Independence

One of the delicate areas of change is regaining some independence. When my family and friends have spent years doing things **for** me, it is hard for them to let go. It is also hard for me to let go of being pampered and served by them. Yet true independence emerges from true interdependent relationships. That's tricky to achieve.

When I was heavier, there were many things I couldn't do. Because of the swelling in my legs, I was given very tight support stockings to wear. Much to my amazement, I could not bend over enough to get these on. My husband had to do that for me. While I was being treated for this swelling, I was required to wear nighttime strapping to avoid water gathering in the area of my ankles. I couldn't do that either. My husband did that.

I didn't drive anymore. I told people it was because I was on twelve different medications. That wasn't the truth. I stopped driving because I could no longer fit behind the steering wheel. I had a very difficult time getting myself in and out of the car. The seat belt no longer fit, so even after I got belt extensions from the car dealer, I still found it difficult to be comfortable. There just wasn't enough room.

I could no longer stand and take a shower, and had trouble with many personal tasks that one takes for granted. I used two canes to walk and had to have the car brought right up to me in order for me to get into it. I was often left off right in front of the store so I could hobble with my canes into the store in search of a motorized shopping cart to ride. If a store did not have a cart available, I was no longer interested in shopping. I would sit on a bench while others did the shopping for me.

People opened doors, carried things for me, and gave me sad, sympathetic looks as if to say, "Lady, you are my good deed for the day." And although I appreciated all the valiant efforts on the part of those around me, I longed for the days when I could do some things by myself again.

The Time Is Now

Now things are different for me. Each day I become a little bit braver in attempting to do the things others have done for me in the past. Gently thanking others for their encouragement, I seek to become a bit more interdependent than totally dependent on others.

There are many things I can do for myself now. I can bend over and put on my own stockings in the morning. I can care for my personal needs. I can walk from the handicap parking spaces instead of being dropped off at the store door. I took the car out the other day and drove approximately seventeen blocks to an appointment I had. It was the first time I had driven in almost three years. It felt good to experience that independence. Now when I need to drive, I know that I can because I fit behind the steering wheel without the extension belt. I am now considered a normal size even though I am still obese.

I hadn't gone down into my basement for almost a year because I was afraid I wouldn't make it down and back up the steps. I went into the basement yesterday, could do some cleaning and sorting, and found my way back up the steps. I felt I accomplished a great feat.

I am currently trying to walk in my home without the necessity of my two canes. I am getting better every day. I can walk into church standing tall and feeling good about myself. I feel the delight of the people who have been praying for me and asking their angels to help me.

Every day is a new revelation of the miracles happening inside of me. I speak more confidently, feel more womanly, and am fired up about life. The surgery has made a lot of difference in my quality of life, and I am very grateful for that. I find myself giving thanks to God and the angels, those in heaven and those on earth without wings, who have helped me on this journey.

More Differences

At this writing I am ten months out of surgery and the differences in my life are many. From a medical standpoint, I am taking only two medications instead of twelve. I also take vitamins to reinforce my body system. I use insulin once at night, injecting fifteen units instead of 128 in four injections. My blood pressure, heart health, and cholesterol are doing fine. I have energy to spare, which sometimes surprises those around me.

Spiritually I feel more grounded than ever. There is a place for God and his angels in my life. I call upon them daily to help me thin out the clutter of my life. I beg for simplicity of mind and spirit. I pray for spiritual vision so that I might see what is truly essential to being happy in this world while daydreaming about the wonders of eternity. I find myself inspired to write, to speak, but especially to be compassionate toward those who are in need of a listening ear. I feel the Spirit of God hovering over me, and I am so grateful for God's presence in my life. I know that I am not alone even in the difficult times.

I have a different sense of humor. I find myself laughing more. I feel more joyful because I can see things in perspective. I can give myself the credit due me without thinking of myself as conceited because I know that the gifts come from the God presence within me. I don't have to be the happy fat person anymore. I can be myself … a person who is trying to become the best person I can be.

My friends have been supportive and caring. They ask their questions, respect my decisions, and respect me. They often call me an inspiration because of the choices I have made. However, I know where that strength comes from and I know the temptations I give in to. I am not perfect, but they love me anyway.

The Glow

Many people I haven't seen for a while tell me there is a certain glow about me. I look healthier in my face, and I carry myself with a lot more confidence. I seem younger, is what they say.

Doc was the first to tell me about the glow about my face and head. I thought she was crazy. Then others started to comment using the same words. At first it freaked me out. Then I looked at some pictures of me two years ago and pictures taken today. And I saw the glow.

I try to rationalize by saying it is the camera light, but I now understand that it is the divine presence in me. This presence is in everyone who wants to be connected to the deeper self within. As I watched other people, I could see the glow or aura around them. It is energy waiting to be used for good. The divine God who loves us wants to reside in us. We are to be his dwelling place on earth. I stopped denying the presence of the glow or aura … .and now praise God for the reality of this sign of his love.

The 100 + Party

I needed to say thank you to many people who helped me thus far. So I decided to have a 100+ party. I had lost one hundred pounds and wanted folks to know how grateful I was for their prayers and loving support in the last nine months. I invited them to a party and a healthy meal that I prepared for them.

The night before and morning of the party, we had an awful snow storm. Many of my family and parish friends are elderly, and this meant they had to make a very hard decision to come or not. It was not a safe situation by any means.

I found myself understanding if few people showed. Of course I was disappointed by the weather but realized I could not control that. All of a sudden, as the time for the party drew closer, people started to come. I was so surprised that they would come out in such terrible weather for such an unusual celebration. After all, I never heard of anyone celebrating a weight loss with their friends. The room was filled with family and friends who came to show their continued support for me.

It was important to me to be able to share the journey of the last nine months. I explained the surgery, the hard times I had, my stubbornness, and my total dependence on God, the angels, and my friends' prayers. I needed to tell them how important they were to me and still are. I had kept them informed with my progress with updates after I met with the doctor or physician's assistant. Their emails offered continued support and prayer. I saw in that room the support group that is so necessary for a weight management tool to be successful. I knew what I have known all along: I am not alone. I am loved. I am cared for. I mean a lot to a great many people, and I have a responsibility to keep myself healthy so I can do the work God has called me to do on this earth.

Chapter Thirteen

Spiritual Dependence on God

I need God in my life. I want God in my life. As I experience this time of transition, I realize how I really need to be connected to the Divine Intimacy that is love. My prayer is daily ... sometimes every moment is a cry for help, love, compassion or mercy. Prayer is my connection to the Divine presence. It calls me to go within my heart and to dwell there in peace. I walk with God so as not to stumble in the darkness of my own mind. I ask for the Divine footsteps to lead me, walk beside me and behind me so that I might be protected in all that I do and all that is to come. I am humbled before God for without God's great love and trust in me, I would not be the person I am becoming. I need God in my life.

A Tool, Not a Cure

I have mentioned a number of times that this surgery is a tool for me not a cure. I am still able to make decisions that will increase my success or slow down my weight loss. Every day I need to recommit to doing what the medical staff has advised me to do. Every day I am tempted by the doughnuts in the kitchen or the ice cream in the freezer. I sometimes hear candy bars calling my name. Every meal tempts me to eat more stuff than the valuable protein I need in order to sustain this body in a healthy way. Every day is a challenge that calls me to say YES to life. In saying YES to some things, I must say NO to others.

The Journey Continues

This is one of the hardest journeys I have ever walked. Yet it is probably the most important journey I will ever be asked to walk. It is significant to my continuing to becoming the person I am called to be. Each step is taken with the company of the angels and saints, those in heaven and those on earth who care for me.

I experience a sense of gratitude every morning when my eyes open and I realize I have been gifted with another day of life and love. Each new day is another birthday. It is a celebration of all that can be good and beautiful. Each day holds numerous opportunities for me to experience the world as God intends. Each day is also filled with challenges to keep myself grounded in the love of the Divine One. Each day I am called to the intimacy of prayer and union with God. I am also called to holy leisure, time for myself and space to explore the person I am within. This call is to be renewed and refreshed, basking in the love of a God who holds me tenderly and with great passion. This call is an invitation to leave all darkness behind and to keep focused on the light of God's face. May God grant us all what we need so that we can be the best possible person we can be, and may we always reflect the shining countenance of God to others. May the angels guide us as we continue to walk toward truth.

Chapter Fourteen

Prayers and Reflections

A Prayer to Saint Michael

Archangel Michael,
You defend us in battle against the evil one
Who roams our earth trying to destroy
the hearts of all who yearn for the holy.
Protect us from being defeated by depression and fear.
These only take us away from the love of God.
Equip us with the sword of truth
So that we may cast away the lies and deceit of the
dragon of hatred.
Lift our spirits so that we may rise above the self doubts and
confusion that approach us all in the lonely moments of life.
Help us in these stressful moments to trust God all the more.
Michael, be our safeguard and protect us today and always. Amen.

A Prayer to Saint Raphael

O Healing Angel, Raphael,
Come to my aid and heal me of all the burdens
that I am being asked to bear.
If it is not possible to remove them,
Then walk with me and help me carry them
With faith and trust in the love of the Divine.
May God who called you to help our ancestors
Call you to help as I journey toward Life.
Be my healing companion, today and always. Amen.

A Prayer for All Who Face Addiction

Divine One,
Who loves me and calls me by name,
walk with me this day.
Take my hand as I journey into this new day
full of challenges and choices.
Help me to choose the good.
Help me to choose life for myself so that
I may reflect the love and life you offer all
who seek the good and holy.
Be with me when I am afraid.
Be with me when I am tempted
to be less than what you call me to be.
I offer this day and all it holds to you.
Keep me safe and give me joy. Amen.

When I Cannot Choose the Good

When I cannot choose the good
When I am afraid of saying no
When I want to go back to what I once was,
Help me God, to choose the good.

When I am tired of the discipline
When I want to do what is easy
When I want to give up,
Help me God, to choose the good.

I do not walk alone.
I am not in this all alone.
I have the power to rise above
and choose the good.

Come my angels,
Come to my aid.
Holy men and women of God,
Help me be strong.
And in this hour of need,
Help me to choose the good. Amen.

Challenges

Morning comes and once again
I am challenged
to start my day with hope.
My heart trembles
as I hesitate to even move from my bed.
I am safe here, under warmth of covers
lying in the stillness of the early dawn.
I am safe
as a child resting in his mother's womb.
And I do not want to budge.
But reality calls me to start my day and
so I turn to you, Divine One, to hold me in your care.
As I rise from my safety zone,
help me to know that you rise with me,
holding me in the very palm of your loving hand.
Help me to raise my heart and soul to you
in gratitude for this new day
regardless of what may lie ahead.
You are all I need.
You are my strength.
You walk with me. Amen.

Clay Feet

I often hear how short life is
and how I should be living it to the fullest.
But there are times when I meet folks I just find difficult to love.

I have asked for patience, for compassion, for understanding.
I find myself falling into tolerance instead.
And I feel uncomfortable.

I have clay feet, Lord, and I need your help.
I am no angel.
Let me see in others the gifts they have to offer.
Adjust my attitude.

In those moments when I can't pray for what I should,
Send your Spirit to help me.
Help me to change. Amen.

One Day at a Time

One day at a time.
That's all I can handle.
One small step followed by another
is all I can manage to walk.

Difficulties come and I am afraid
that today will be too much for me to handle.
Then I remember.
That one day at a time is what I have to give.
One day at a time is all that is asked of me.

In the moments when I feel
hesitant to move into the future,
help me to remember the present moment.
Help me to embrace the now.

Let your angels remind me that one day is like a thousand years
and a thousand years is like one day with You.
Time is not my time but yours.
You are pleased with my daily walk.
Help me to be pleased as well. Amen.

Waiting

How I hate to wait.
How I long to have changes come quickly.
But that is not reality.
That is not the way life is.

Yet you Lord, wait for me.
You are always waiting for me to come to my senses.
You are always waiting for me to admit the truth.
You are always waiting for me to open my heart to newness.

How I hate to wait.
How I long to have changes come quickly.
Give me patience, Lord,
that changes that come will be real and lasting.
And in your timing. Amen.

Finding Peace

I've heard others say
peace comes when we are in harmony with the world.
I have no reason to doubt that except that I don't feel it.
My heart longs to know the truth of life.
My soul longs to know the path to follow.
My spirit longs to reach to heights of inner solitude that
resides in the depth of my own person.

I cannot reach down into the core by myself.
I don't know how and I am afraid.
Angels of God,
journey with me into the valley of death.

Help me to die to self.
Help me to resurrect the joyful self that I know lies somewhere
in the bondage of fear and anxiety.

Transform my attitude.
Transform my fears into the glory of freedom.
And in that freedom help me to be who I am meant to be.
Help me find peace.

Friends

Thank you, Lord, for friends.
Each day I meet situations that I think I can't handle.
Then I remember those people you put into my life
who believe in me and trust in my gifts.
They challenge me and depend on me to keep going.

My friends reflect your image.
They touch me with hands that heal.
They console me with words of encouragement.
They share your presence so I can endure the pain.
They touch my heart because you have touched theirs.

Lord, help me to appreciate the friends you have given me.
Help me not take anyone for granted.
Teach me to strive to be faithful
to the invitation to be a good friend in return.

Help me to remember, Lord, that you are my best friend.
You are always with me and ready to assist.
Because of your love, I can face today with hope. Amen.

Thanks for My Yes

God of my life,
Thank you for the Yes I could say today.
Thank you for my YES to what is right and good for me.
Thank you that I could put myself first today and care about me.
Thank you for the joy I feel in knowing
I could take small steps towards larger goals.
Thank you for being God of my life. Amen.

I Dance with God

I dance with God
Early morning when the sun greets me.
My arms lift to heaven,
The blue sky blankets my vision
And I sing praise as the dance begins.

I dance with God
As early birds sing their song high above me.
I join the swaying trees that offer praise
As brother wind gently cradles
Their branches and leaves.

I dance with God
As I look at the faces of others
Angels in disguise anxious to begin their day.
I lift my heart and leap for joy
For life has sprung forth anew
And the dancing is a promise forevermore.

Soooooooooo Tired

Lord, you call me,
just as you called the prophets of old.
You call me.
And I am not sure why.

I try to do the work you ask of me.
But, sometimes I get so tired.
It is hard to put one foot in front of the other.
It is as if each step is a workout in itself.

As I go about my tasks today,
be my inspiration.
Send a little extra energy my way
so that all I do is done
with a generous heart.

Give me a sense of zeal to love others and to move
beyond my own needs and wants.
And teach me to take the moments I need to rest
in your arms and be refreshed. Amen.

Trust

Today let me walk in trust
Of the power of good over evil,
The power of love over hatred.

Today let me believe
That this day can be different,
Filled with meaning and joy.

Today let me know that I am guided
By angelic light that shatters the darkness
And brings me to a sense of peace.

Today let trust be the word
That moves me to respond to life
And experience each moment as gift.

The Mountain Top

Come to the mountain top.
It's a deeper view from here.
Release my worries and fears.
Give me balance to stand strong.

Fill me with a song of joy and praise.
Create a sense of gratitude in my heart
for every gift you give.

Let me sing a song of hope.
Let me sing a song of love.
Let me live a song of praise.

Let today be a new day.
Let today be a new beginning. Amen.

About the Author

Jo Therese Fahres grew up in Milwaukee, Wisconsin, the youngest of nine children. Childhood experiences of abuse led her into a life of food addiction. Her obesity resulted in health issues that slowly strangled the quality of life from her. Poor decisions increased her immobility and dependence on others. Then the moment of truth came. Her choice was clear: either pursue the truth or surely die at a young age.

Thinning with the Angels is the story of her journey toward truth. Together with a God who loves unconditionally, Jo Therese was able to choose life again by overcoming a number of adversities. With her faith in the Divine Presence and in the angelic assistance that God provides to all human beings, Jo Therese was able to walk through dark periods of despair and find hope again.

Jo Therese has worked in church ministry for over thirty years. She has written for *Children Celebrate,* a program of Pflaum Publishing Group that shares the Sunday Scripture readings with children. She currently serves as Director of Child Ministry at St. Gregory the Great Catholic Church, where she has worked for the past twenty-two years. Jo Therese has served as acting Spiritual Director for Third Order Lay Franciscan Groups. She facilitates days of prayer and reflection, recently speaking at the Milwaukee Archdiocesan Council of Christian Women Day of Reflection. She has taught both elementary and high school art and theology for twelve years in Milwaukee.

Jo Therese holds a Bachelor of Arts degree in Art Education and Religious Studies and a Master's Degree in Religious Studies from Cardinal

Stritch University in Milwaukee. She also studied at the Franciscan Institute of St. Bonaventure's University in New York.

Jo Therese has been married to her husband Jerry for 27 years. They are the proud parents of two young adults, Anthony and Therese. A resident of Milwaukee, Wisconsin, Jo Therese is an avid fan of the Milwaukee Brewers and the Green Bay Packers.

I have an addiction to food. My addiction brought me to a weight of 400 pounds and I was faced with the truth that continuing at this weight I would surely die at a young age. Trying to live in a body this size was extremely difficult and limited my enjoyment of life. I could barely look myself in the mirror. Depression set in.

I am a new person full of energy and renewed health. The loss of 120 plus pounds has put more bounce in my step and joy in my life. I am grateful to God and the angels, my family and friends, and the doctors and staff who helped me to choose life again. I am not where I want to be but I am on my way!

What Others are Saying about

Thinning with the Angels

This book will speak to your heart and soul while reminding you what wise healers have always known: spiritual energy and health are inseparable. Jo Therese reveals the missing link in the practice of contemporary allopathic medicine by sharing her personal journey out of the darkness of morbid obesity and into the light of renewed health and wellness with the assistance of her angels. The greatest lessons from her personal journey are not so much about what she lost, but in what she gained. She is a beacon of hope, light, wisdom, and truth to all those seeking to find their way out of morbid obesity.

— Dr. Cindy Solliday-McRoy

I picked up this manuscript thinking it was just another book about how to lose weight. Boy, was I wrong! It is an experience that is down to earth and very thought provoking about the battle with one person's journey to control her addiction of food. Jo Therese had to plunge to the very bottom in order to start her struggle up her personal Mt. Everest. Her story is told with a honesty that is compelling, and it makes the reader want to cheer for her hard work. This is a must read for all who suffer from personal demons of addiction and for those who love them. Inspiring!

— Judy Rechlitz

Negative events in our lives can trap us in destructive routines and addictions. *Thinning with the Angels* is an accurate description of one person's struggle with addictions. For the author, time and patience, but especially faith and love, helped to break down those destructive routines, and continue to be a source of great strength in dealing with those addictions.

— Cindy Bremeier

Thinning with the Angels is an account of great struggle, of failure and success, of defeat and victory. It is told with a depth of honesty and insight that can touch the heart of anyone who has ever wrestled with problems that seem overwhelming, of anyone who has ever sailed close to the edge of despair. More importantly, it is a story that can lend hope and comfort, that can inspire courage. Well done, Jo Therese Fahres. Well done.

— Sister Nelda Hernandez, S.D.S.

Letting go OR taking command—Fahres' life struggles are a gripping reflection of those that each of us face. Her step-by-step success with obesity and diabetes challenge my openness to welcome God's healing through the people around me.

Lord Jesus and Your Angels,
Bless Jo Therese Fahres for opening my heart through her life struggle!

— Sheri Masiakowski, Director of Music
St. Gregory the Great Parish, Milwaukee

It's never about the food, or the cigarettes, or the drugs, or many times the violence. It's the way we cope. No one should have to endure what Jo Therese encountered; the food is the way she coped. We silence and stifle our feelings with our drug of choice. It is our protection and attempt to find comfort against what has taken place in our lives. Unfortunately, this can lead to illness and even death. We can present with physical symptoms of headaches, ulcers, cancers, heart disease, and obesity. Our lives are then a series of doctor visits, medications, and other treatments. It's not enough to just treat our symptoms— we must look at our entire being. When one part of our body, mind or spirit is suffering, we are vulnerable. Congratulations to you, Jo Therese, for all the accomplishments made thus far. Continue to exercise—it releases the feel-good brain chemicals— and continue make healthy food choices. You are in control. You then will continue to see a decrease in the need for medications. You are a perfect example of how faith, hard work, and determination can return you to optimal health and well-being. Keep traveling your journey with the Angels.

— Sue Wroblewski, R.N.

Thinning with the Angels is the first-person narrative of one person's tastes at the buffet called Life. As with all smorgasbords, some tastes linger and some pass quickly. Though some foods are healthy for us, others may taste good but not nourish is, while still others make us ill. Jo Therese Fahres invites us to listen to how she has been fed and mis-fed, nourished and undernourished, weakened and finally strengthened at a banquet that eventually brings her to a balanced diet of God's love and presence.

— Fr. Joseph Juknialis, Author